S0-AES-522

OF GODS & STRANGERS

Also by Tina Chang

Poetry
Half-lit Houses (2004)

As Editor
Language for a New Century: Contemporary Poetry from the Middle East, Asia, and Beyond (2008), co-edited with Nathalie Handal and Ravi Shankar

OF GODS & STRANGERS

Tina Chang

Four Way Books
Tribeca

Copyright © 2011 by Tina Chang
No part of this book may be used or reproduced in any manner
without written permission except in the case of brief quotations
embodied in critical articles and reviews.

Please direct all inquiries to:
Editorial Office
Four Way Books
POB 535, Village Station
New York, NY 10014
www.fourwaybooks.com

Library of Congress Cataloging-in-Publication Data

Chang, Tina.
  Of gods & strangers / Tina Chang.
      p. cm.
  Poems.
  ISBN 978-1-935536-17-8 (pbk. : alk. paper)
  I. Title. II. Title: Of gods and strangers.
  PS3603.H3574O4 2011
  811'.6--dc22

                          2011004085

This book is manufactured in the United States of America
and printed on acid-free paper.

Four Way Books is a not-for-profit literary press. We are grateful for the assistance
we receive from individual donors, public arts agencies, and private foundations.

This publication is made possible with public funds
from the National Endowment for the Arts

and from the New York State Council on the Arts, a state agency.

Special thanks to the Jerome Foundation for its generous support of this publication.

Distributed by University Press of New England
One Court Street, Lebanon, NH 03766

We are a proud member of the Council of Literary Magazines and Presses.

[clmp]

CONTENTS

I. REIGN

II. INFINITE AND PLAUSIBLE

III. TERRITORY

For Claude

I. REIGN

SUPERNOVA

I.   The war had been lifted by its roots and transported into
        a book of knives, imitating the sleeptalk of priests.

II.   Sirens sounded and czars gave speeches beneath peach trees.

III.   Noise and crank of the first ships sailed up to the rotting deck
        and anchored down.

IV.   Jeeps crossed the field filled with rebels, black scarves
        smothered half their faces.

V.   The president in a bulletproof car gloved and waving, a sea
        parts for no one, the populace sits as crows on sidewalks
        and front steps, mouths moving.

VI.   We think they are saying one thing. They are really saying
        another.

VII.   The war of religions without disciples had been waging
        for over a decade.

VIII.   During the last summer the lungs of the priests and
        politicians had blossomed into a thin blue flame.

IX.   The gods packed their belongings and trekked to find work,
        forage for food. Starving, their bodies cracked open and
        someone said they saw the past in that interior.

X.   Pinned on the mouths of visionaries were pink petals or flesh
        as seen from a distance with binoculars.

XI.   The tangle of mortals and the tangle of immortals were not
        of this world.

XII.   It is the Asian fable of the child who had wandered too far
        from home and found peaches that she placed in the pockets
        of her skirt. She gathered so many, they weighed her down.
        She grew tired and fell into a deep sleep. When she woke
        the peaches had sprouted into new kingdoms.

XIII.   These stories and others were memorized by kings.

XIV.   When interrogated, the store clerks and vendors said they knew nothing.

XV.   The peaches vanished. All the stories were folded into napkins and placed neatly into drawers.

XVI.   In secret rooms, men with shirt sleeves rolled up made a different kind of mythology. On typewriters, letters seared into paper. Ding of the bell when the carriage returned.

XVII.   All night cigarette butts fell from their red wicks.

XVIII.   There were many different writers. It was not a quickly written book.

XIX.   The book moved in real time.

ATLAS

I.   It had been many years since anyone heard the turn of the key of the immortals so they forgot what had been promised them.

II.   No one knew of the underground prisons that had been built and what happened there.

III.   The noises were not human.

IV.   The first lady gestured to herself on the front lawn and peaches rolled to her feet. They were devoured by the pet spaniel, a beloved mascot.

V.   All the chapters were either destroyed, catalogued, combined with other texts.

VI.   There was confusion over its origin and conclusion.

VII.   The heretics stayed up into the night to sew flags that were placed on boats headed to the great new world.

VIII.   One of the boats was a funeral pyre.

IX.   Love burned inside a building. No one jumped. No one thought of jumping.

X.   History stayed locked in that room.

XI.   The rearrangement of the world took time.

XII.   So the handwriting and analyzing were slow.

XIII. As the trees split, a religion crashed to a moan.

XIV.   People were shocked to learn the sky was not a chariot
       of water.

XV.   The soul of the country rolled into the Indian Ocean.

XVI.   The eyes of the good men fell from their seats and scattered
       as marbles on the city streets. Citizens stumbled and broke
       their knees.

XVII. The ears of the soldiers had become closed factories
       and there was no one to hear truth rowing a damaged boat
       through waves.

XVIII. Until what were known as the great savages came.
       One of them I took to loving.

XIX.   So much cracked porcelain after the conflict, history's white
       bowls laid smashed, pieces rocking. So many riches the king
       didn't care to take when he escaped: wind-up dragon breathed
       mechanical fire, a toy peacock with metallic feathers chimed.

XX.   The gods had another plan.

XXI.   Why am I thinking of my lovers now?

XXII. Smashed down.

POLARIS

I.   Someone is blindfolded. A robe burns and takes off into
       a flock of swallows.

II.   Each man knocks on the door of the future and hears
       an avalanche of women charging back.

III.   His tongue pushed into the plush of mine and its difficult
       bedding.

IV.   The sky separated into sheets of paper, torn leaf from leaf.

V.   I bent the corners of the pages to keep my place in history.
        As if a kind of faith were in the saving.
VI.   My irreconcilable past spread its wings through a failed life
        to the one that succeeded it.
VII.   Rush of leaves on water. Flurry of paper money.
VIII.   Then the book was written again.
IX.   Then the book was never finished.
X.   Quiet.
XI.   No noise.
XII.   We call this aftermath.
XIII.   We call it end.
XIV.   Before beginning.
XV.   My hand over your mouth.
XVI.   You want to smash me.
XVII.   You're angry.
XVIII. You are writing the book too.
XIX.   You are the author now.
XX.   Your signature, lover, goes here _____

LUCIDA

I.   You are pledging allegiance.
II.   Some say they gave up their mothers. Some say they gave up
        a son.
III.   Some say they never would.
IV.   You never know.
V.   We lost track of time. We found our calling.
VI.   Entered the house.
VII.   What followed was a constant urging.
VIII.   The text had to leave.
IX.   You would not allow it so the text and I stayed.

X. The book had been written long ago and left on the bank
of the river.
XI. You were my greatest love and the most luminous things
are said that simply.
XII. The book was written in the space between us.
XIII. Horizontal and vertical, space between soil and sky.
XIV. Once the pages were free falling and someone collected them
from the ground, bound them with a steady hand.
XV. And the rummaging that we found.
XVI. You took the pages and kissed them. Willed them to be.
XVII. You placed the book back. Our names were there.
XVIII. You did not see the names but I knew they were there
in the ledger of the living.
XIX. Tangle of mortal to mortal.
XX. God to god.

EMPRESS DOWAGER BOOGIES

Last night I found my face below
the water in my cupped hands.

The mask made of copper and bone
criss-crossing to make a smirk,

a false glamour, a plated glaze.
I unwound myself from the heavy

machinery of my body's burden.
The lute, the light, chime.

I'll get up and partner myself
with music, the purple moon

peeling itself like a plum.
Men stand in a circle and

they will ask and ask again.
I want to pick the thick bud,

to lose myself in the body's posture
bending in or away, to let

my majesty and birthright go
and gesture toward a waking life.

DOWAGER IN MATRIMONY

What is calling? Does it sound like a sick bird
or a gramophone playing in the back room?

I'm in a chamber breathing, satin winds a whittled torso,
a face powdered so rouge it becomes an empire.

My stepmother wraps my feet, cracking my bones
bending them to crushed birds inside a hollow shelter,

fitted, doused with fire. The blue has been stolen
from outside and placed inside my mouth like a fog.

A pitcher is poured over my hair and rushes
to the floor in an invisible dress. I bend, teeter.

Look at my countenance, look at it fading.
The blood failing to work when the body is not blind,

but hungry.

*

Listen carefully.

*

Today is the last and final day before my wedding.
Tomorrow I will die in a wooden sedan made especially for me.

There will be servants on either side as I'm carried
to a crystalline water. All around me leaves fall red, red, red,

gold. Put a finger to my lip and see if the animal
will sip or bite back. I am boxed, perfumed,

sutured for a royal coronation. *Heaven's Mouth* is the place
I name my room. I lock myself in as the servants

run frantically to find the key. The key that fit, the key
that entered, the key. Miles away, peonies on a balcony

that haven't been watered in years. They survive.
There is a high stone wall and I live behind it.

I peer through a hole in the universe in the days I travel
nowhere. Hot water steaming. I'll take my bath, pure sheen and glow.

Her dress rose up and covered her frightened face as she fell.
One finger of God touches me so gently on the mouth.

Just a little gesture like a gulp, a twitter. Glass body
on the torn sheets. I never made a sound when he entered the room.

BOOK

I could make a book of it, out of ash. Or maybe it would be more
like a recipe where we pound it to dough with our firm hands,
then roll it up into a tear shape and drop it into hot oil.

The other day I dreamed that I had the courage to leave you.
But you became an expert herdsman. You put the saddle on me
and reigned me in for good. We couldn't get close enough so we moved

to another room, a windowless one. Getting there was like being lost,
change jingling in your pockets, yesterday's cash, folded wet bills, cigarettes.
You said in the new year maybe you'd settle for just one person.

On the dance floor, I remember your heart's pound and whistle
through a small hole hollowed out just for me. It will matter someday.
Everything that happened between us, the absence too. After

we were done, there was fruit. Impossible to break, but you tore it open
anyway, drilled inside with your fingers. You found the seed and ate
that too. Juices dripping, the rind reeling like a wild tongue in ruin.

SELF-PORTRAIT AS IMAGINARY DJ

You can take no more thunder when the key turns
and it's another man, breaking in like a thief.
He is not a thief, but a murderer. Not
a murderer, but a soul bitten on the side.

You harpoon the heart, furious with the time
it took to love, to make decisions. There was
a slip of paper from God wedged under your door.
Some say it was a rejection notice, some say

it was a love letter penned in the middle of the night
when he couldn't sleep. That ancient script,
no signature. At the penny arcade, you place a coin
into the machine, watch an image of a vixen

slowly take off her coat like a religion,
letting down her hair, tresses that swing
to the left before they still, the movements
black and white, staccato.

Pout, sway of her legs peaking from her skirt.
Your eyes are pressed into the viewing glass, the penny
runs out before the last piece of clothing falls.
All that expectation, waiting for that last garment

to be taken off, mortal remnants and music.
There's a twin of you who strides into a bar outside
of city limits, who orders a shot under a disco ball,
who answers to a name that is not her own.

THE EMPRESS DREAMS AFTER A POISONED MEAL

Once the guards sprayed me down unclothed
I left my veil in a pool of my own waking
A pomegranate ruptured in my sleep, stains
under my fingernails and on my ghost gown
when I rose my maid played the music of my tragic
birth I miss my husband's summoning harmony
swirling I am always alone Documents
confirm I had many different names and official
stamps that said I was born I exhale smoke
signals through a haze A throat raw from yawning
feet bruised from tripping through the green maze
Soon the mechanical toys and windup clocks
will be smashed and shot in the Summer Palace
Oh the jewels hairpin of plum blossoms
ring of dragonfly circling above this chipped crown
Bring the gems into my room on someone's back
Let me model all my bracelets that anchor me
to this empire In the courtyard I am a cat mewing
with my collar on fed with imperial poison I sleep
curled at the center filled with lion dogs sniffing
as if I were historical food I never minded My
kingdom one world beneath me My sleeping sound

THE FULL FACES OF DOGS ARE BARKING

as if hunger were the destination, the great ambition.
What we needed most was to get to the very center.
We ate and ate, getting greedier as the night wore on.
We smoked and drank until there was nothing left

to take, after all was salted and sated. The last thing
to do was to fall asleep, the body so spent, it lay
in exhaustion like a flat tire. That felt like truth
but it was more threatening. I once saw a dying horse

on the side of the road and hoped it knew some kind
of great pleasure before this, its large brown eyes wet
and expiring. We take what we need with nothing
to spare. Unless there's air.

PATRIOTISM

The village was in tatters, smoking before it spoke,
shrapnel in a lung, a toothache in a guilty mouth.

There's something in the back of my mind I'd like
to remember, rubble there and a shovel for digging.

We stood in the deep muck for years. I wrote
love notes to nurse him back to health. If he dreamed

origami cranes I kept folding this paper inward
and inward until it bloomed and found velocity.

To get inside the earth's black center, I must have tools.
I must be alert and willful. I sat on the ground

to get down deeper, below kneeling, below bowing
and scramble, and boulder. And when you get that low,

you can mount the cry, the zero. What happened
in the marriage between the heart and its territory?

The tools were man-made, the tools worked slowly with labor.
The work was not without toil. When I found him there

face up, I put my mouth to his mouth, exhaled
for many years, my tongue waving like a flag.

LOVE

I am haunted by how much our mothers do not know.
How a republic falls because of its backhanded deals,
stairwell secrets. My mother does not know I am lying
with a man who is darker than me, that we do not
have names for how we truly treat our bodies.
What we do with them. The other possesses me.
Without him the perception of me fails to exist.
My mother now is taking her sheers and cutting
through live shrimp. When I was a child she peeled
each flushed grape until only the pale fleshy bead
remained. She placed them onto a plate in one shining
mound, deseeded, in front of me. How I sucked and bled
the fruit of all their juice, hypnotized in front of the buzz
of television in each version of my childhood. I am
her daughter. This is certain. I am lying down with a man
who is darker than me and maybe this poem is my
real republic, my face is my face, or is it stolen from
my mother and hung over mine? If I were a dream
you could say my countenance was a string of flickering lights
made of teeth or an expression unraveling like a carpet
into a narrow river of another life. Does truth matter
when it's floating face up or face down?
The answer to this makes all the difference.

STILL LIFE: *ALCOHOL AND PEARS*

Un.

You were mixed in with the paintings.
A good man with a cornucopia of fruits
to the left, stained window shade
to the right. The odor of malt, the muted
flavor when it spilled down. Outside,
a pastoral setting. Inside the painting
there is nowhere for you to sit, so you pose
as bartender, lean by the counter and pour
the gin, put on a scratched record
which becomes part of the scene and,
did I mention, you're also the painter.

Deux.

A citywide brown-out when the body
was a holy box. When you entered at night,
the tragic scent. Clothes removed,
shirt laid neatly next to the shoes.
Your face was the moon damaged by air,
someone sleeping beneath you thought
you were her father singing. But
there was no singing. No song at all.
The notes carried over to his death
and nightwatch, across lamplight into casket.

Trois.

It's as if you're a survivor from a plane crash,
FIGURE 1 lifted from metal, ash and buckle,
a black box of voices that will disclose every secret
after everyone is gone. We can still hear them
pleading as if in the midst of flight someone
had authority over each destiny. Sketches
were left of the night you were found:
Someone offers you a drink and sees you
for the first time. When you're ready to be recognized,
the head tips back. Swallow the translucence,
tinted neon with ice, melting into a flash flood.

Four.

The best gesture is left for last. If we stay
in this room, we won't be found. Paint brushes
dry next to the knots of necklaces, wine leaks,
a chandelier swings like an arm. The bell is a bell
that stays mute when left unpressed. It is obedient,
good. The door is a door that does not open
for anyone. If you were a real artist you would have
remembered more about the sweat and the way
it calmly carved its way into the bedpost. The way
the shutters could unfasten and open out to the
great pastoral. A dangerous thunder, living is.

SELF-PORTRAIT AS EMPRESS DOWAGER

I met you at the crossroad, at the coronation
when pink chrysanthemums shattered
on the long carpet. I bowed through

the onslaught of snow and petals.
Your long nails fanned out, singed sparked air.
I continued to rise in folds of orange.

I was almost a legend, a soldier,
so you had me carry you as footman.
I was low and humble, a steady, threadbare

servant. I was beat and rhythm marching
behind you, holding your coat, your sail,
opening myself to your perfumed commands.

At night, I pulled the curtains back, opened you,
a tinier armor than I imagined with a wind-up
clock at the center, a few chimes, then I drank

a little poison before I crawled in, hunkered down
on my haunches. I uncovered my tusks and my weapons,
cleaned the hollows, undid your mane of hair, unwrapped

the crown from your temple, readying myself
for anonymity, invisibility, grandeur and bliss.
Tonight I wear my lipstick like a mouthpiece.

Love, I am worshipful of the source. It is a well,
it feels like water, it is colorless but I taste it.
I build a house for my new desire with wide windows

hammered. There's my body crashing out, not
the younger self I knew, unrecognizable before
my tenth name was given, when one chrysanthemum

fought to be alive. Today it is my earth's time
and earth's minute. I switch on the blue current
with my delicate finger, a high order from on high.

I DEMAND YOU KNOW MY FLYING

You who allow yourself to touch down,
no mad Icarus but just a woman.

That's freedom. No longer needing
to be cosmic, goddess among gods.

It's okay to lower, to lounge,
to lie with eyes closer to the base,

rock bottom, beneath sea,
to get deeper to form and its

function, below water level,
the whale, the shark fin, delve.

You're at the earth's hot core,
lower than that, you're in bed

sleeping soundly after a night
on the Lower East Side, lower

and you've hunted yourself down,
beast locked inside your beast heart,

disco music, old school music,
you've gotten past it, the lyric

nonsensical now, *la la la* went
the thick chords when you ripped

the song out of the earth's throat
and slept with it and you hummed

and it hummed back.

CUTTING IT DOWN

Trotsky died with a blow from an axe.
The night before his demise, Kahlo leaned into him,
took one of her famous roses from her hair
and placed it in his lapel. He laid his head down

between her breasts, needing her shocking color,
her feasts and white frocks. He kissed her
swollen mouth, her lips crowned by tender
black hair. He sought a version of his life

past border where Frida floated above him,
extinct in her shadow, her bed in flames.
At night a deer inhabited her body, lit eyes
possessing the animal. In a self-portrait

she held her own twin's hand, one who was
laden down by tradition, another freed from it,
the forced embrace and cleaved tongue flicking
like a serpent's. When God multiplied the soul,

it fractured, splintered beast wandering in the mirror,
strangeness of pleasure in tandem. What does that say
about the spirit, one's own disaster split in two,
to halve the pain or double it?

BAGUIO

Each one calls the other crazy bent down to tend a bright need.
The butchers with their smeared aprons croon with knives.

The dog's face hovers, skin lighter than you would imagine
unraveling like transparent paper, halos stacked in a corner.

I listen to the expert humming of the butcher who sings
while he cuts. I would like to think that we did not come here

to say goodbye. My leaving you is the swinging single bulb above
these bones where I remember myself in this alleyway with you.

I am averaging that I love you best once the animal has been stripped,
teeth bare, meat singing too. I imagine the pig's face and the cow's face

existing side by side on the farm beyond this town. Their blank stares
as they are shepherded into the truck. I want to go to Cebu tomorrow.

Instead, we'll ride in air-conditioned taxis. Instead, we will watch
the maid wax the floor with a monstrous machine.

That day we fought, the rains came down and I rode a jeepney
alone through a city I didn't know. What is this force

that makes me continually lost? What is it that I want
in all these disappearing cities? One street led to another

until it was night, until I got off with bags in my arms, food in cartons,
sauces dripping, stumbling in the direction of my great need.

THE EMPRESS DOWAGER HAS ONE BIRD

Soldered to her finger, I feast
on flecks of gold. I am a torch lit,
a flame glowing beneath a wing tip.
It's like nesting in the voicebox.
A call of self to self. It is not
kindness, but compassion. Not
admiration, but recognition.
A birdcage with hinges squeaking
inward. I've learned to hold still
on her painted nail, a long arching
branch, paid lover on a bed.

BITCH TREE

I was sitting on the bitch tree, smirky and small.
Just me to myself with my hats on, a tulle dress
eating pomegranates, throwing seeds, as the sun rose
and fell into my body's mouth. There were no boo hoos
but murmurs and people far below grew distant.
Money fell out of the tree, honey formed the sap,
spectators took photos as if a magic was to start.

And none could capture my face when film met silver,
only a halo around the bitch tree but not
the expression of the maker. Yes, I balked
and said, I never had a father, threw weather
in the hard rain, my face a faucet hurling down
and still I sat on the branch, murdering berries
with my fruit mouth, then became silent when it was night.

No one was there to examine the bitch who shifted
and grimaced only when there was an audience.
An urge for urgency, my soul hangs like a puppet,
knocks between my lungs, bends to the song of the sister
peach tree: Love me when all the ripe clusters drop.
I remembered my job and shook the leaves and howled
like a monkey, wanting the next weather, next
instant, that high lightning barking from the boughs.

SEX GOSPELS

1.

For days I've been looking for you to reach
to me as you did in our other life. Four whiskeys later,
there is a gun. It made me reel, thought of your grasp
on metal, the trigger, no bullets, square of light
through the half-closed window. People go about
their own business on the street. I am inside with
a different belief in hunger, licking the residue
of anything left inside me that was good or worth saving.

2.

There was dynamite and a well.
I had gone there to hoist the bucket,
hear the squeak of the pulley bringing
the fresh water up. You held explosives
and threw them in like a bundle of branches.
Never a sound when it happened, just a vacuum,
the earth's inhale, and you took me in
and let me slide down the hollow eye.

3.

Time so domestic, it lay on its side like a dog.
Garments dissolve in the ferocious light
by the bureau, the couch in the corner.
You pull me aside as you enter, after your
long day's work, suited, the knot in your tie
fully wound. I am making my awful dinner
of peas and gray steak. A rush, a flutter of papers

on the desk, no words or graces, rummage for flight.
We tear them down, the curtains, topple the chairs.
And when it is over, heaving, clinks from the fireplace
as if pigeons were caught inside the flue, a sound
that startled me when I lifted my ear from the floor.

4.

Unbuckle the belt, thud as it falls. A path.
Heat moving through now. The horse keeps
coming back. Its long face, long torso.
I curse at it. It stays.

5.

I've watched the train move in me. 35 years through
New York, Pittsburgh, Maryland, DC, Taiwan,
India, Tunisia. I'll arrive home by evening, breathing
through my one good heart. Invisible bandits stand
by the tracks ready to take what we value most. You walk
in my future, instructions memorized for my destiny,
blueprint of the locomotive as we slip through canyons.
You serve me tea and biscuits before I retire. Lie down
in my berth, shut the curtains like a shroud. I'll utter
the names of men before you and mistake you for them
in the dark. We will tangle and there will be no way
to tell us apart. The night train is a current running
until there is no fuel. I am moving farther away from
that essential home. The train doesn't remember the stops
it passed. Only minds the wind and that it must exceed it.

6.

When we were born, there were twin lightning
storms on opposite sides of the earth.
White birds colliding into black birds that high.

7.

I had run out of fortune and still sought to own.
You had a roll of damp bills mixed with your matches.
If there was music, it was gospel. New words
I had learned that year, chords I held long enough
to remember their element. I sniffled from cold,
my coat not sufficient. You searched inside the pockets
wanting me to taste the smoke in your mouth.
The train passes blocks away but the sound near enough
to feel humming in my marrow. At the intersection
the traffic light changes as the sun alters its color too,
the insistence staining sky and all, crashing
in every direction and then melting down, God's
shattered body in the wild, blackening the dark.

TOWARD DIVINITY

I poked out an eye so the saved eye
could see, like a Cyclops with a vision,
the storm clouds moved in, soft
and faithless, burning in every pattern.
I made this world for Myself so when
the waters came, I laid my face down
to the sand. Nights like this, diamonds
melt. Glaciers shift and sink.
I'm up all night pulling levers, filling
buckets and poking pinpricks in the sky
with scissors. Let the hail come.
I'll create a tree and speak into it,
make it move feminine, in the wind.
I'll take the branches in my arms and weep.
In the morning, the clouds will cry back
into my face. When I grow up,
I'll put my hands in the air and breathe
heavenward and just like that I'll be free.

CHARLATAN, SELF-STYLED

Shorn of hair, washed, purple, a woman

beginning. Mark of the fox, baby smooth,

wooden spoon, a man, an opposite. I have

nearly boiled myself in a brew to start again,

had my girls mix up a tincture of new me

in a new era. I shine having risen

from the bottom, the soles

of my feet still smoldering.

II. INFINITE AND PLAUSIBLE

WILD INVENTION

This is a story about a girl who ran
all night after the wolf, aimed
at its hind legs, then stood above it
shot it between the eyes, skinned it
until the soul of the animal departed
from this world. Then the meat
stopped pulsing, then it shined
with all its delicate possibilities.

The girl stalked the forest with nothing
but a shotgun and compass, due north,
hollowed the animal under moonlight,
desire dripped blood into a tin pan,
the stars leaked a tonic into her cup.
Her appetite was the forest she traveled.
Though lost, she dragged the wolf with her,
a past surrendering to a new life. The sun
emerged over the mountain like a heart
flayed open with a light in the middle.

*

The animal must be shot. You must
be hungry enough to skin it without
flinching, must be willing to cook it,
still trembling over the watchful eye
of the fire. You must also be willing
to track yourself down, kneel beside
the will of a maker who made all beasts
fear for their end. The rabbit quivers

in its white coat, raises its ears and takes
off. The boar bursts from its hind legs
escaping the hillsides. You eat, grateful
for the skin that keeps this life intact
under the roof beams of your long life,
under a bridge that is a heaven of deer bones.
You are a more wonderful animal
than you could ever imagine: great flying
loon. Foxes coupling in the dark brush.

TINY SOULS

They are here now, in the human world,
black instruments pointed toward targets

tunneling through grace. Ruin, the most real
and palpable conclusion. It is leveled, face down.

Ruin gets up. Once brushed off, it glows.
There are moments when I no longer live

in the future tense. I walk forward as if I am
limitless. The angels come to impart a message

as they scribble on brick, revise the landscape.
Grace is an arrow shot through air. It hits a surface

and the surface hums. It rises and lifts above
the crosshatch of collapse. I believe this hope

is a table I dance on. This country is not
on the map. This place known for its bad

presidents, poor plumbing, misdirected people.
We are using this as a blueprint. A nation

of insomniacs, we sit on stoops listening to one
radio station: *testing, testing* in the humid air.

EVOLUTION OF DANGER

I'm the one in the back of the bar, drinking cachaça,
fingering the lip of the glass. Every dream has left
me now as I wait for the next song: Drag and drum.
They'll be no humming in this room, only fragrance
of sweat and fuel. To make the animal go. To make it
Hungry. After that there is Thirst.

*

I danced in the border town until it wasn't decent,
until I was my grandest self hitchhiking, my slim arm
out like the stalk of a tired flower, waving, silver rings
catch the headlights. I'm not sure what I wanted
as we rode on his motorcycle where Chinese signs blurred
past, flashing red, then blue, and I breathed in the scent
of fish and plum. My hands found their way to his pockets
as I rode without helmet, careening toward the cemetery,
the moon dripping light onto avenues of tombstones.

*

If the Tunisian black market was hidden within a maze.
If I couldn't find my way, I asked. The wide eyes
of the boy who led me to the Mediterranean Sea.
If I took his kindness as a version of truth and stood
posing for a photo in front of bicycles leaned
against the sand colored walls. If I arrived
at the center of the market, women in black muslin
sold glazed tile on blankets. When I bent down,

the men surrounded me. If they asked for money
I had nothing. If they threw their bills around me,
I recall the purple and red faces crushed on paper.

*

Attempting to cross the border with no passport,
no money. The contents had fallen out of her
pocket as she ran for the bus. She made promises
to the officers, bared an inner thigh until their eyes
grew wide, until they stamped a sheet of official paper
with tri-colored emblems. The man's fist
was large though it twitched as he pounded
the stamp onto the translucent page. The little
money she had inside an orange handkerchief tied
to her hair, coins rolling to the ground as she fled.

*

Perhaps it was chance that I ended on the far side
of the earth. Atrocities of our entanglement not on the bed
but beside it. Using our mouths as tools for betterment,
for seduction, for completion. The vertebrae twist
into a question mark to conform to another's.

In the Patanal, the cowboys steadied the horses
in the barn, one animal's labored breathing, the sigh
as the coarse brush worked through the mane.
The owner's daughter learned to move her hips
as she practiced her samba before the steaming pot,
and radio clicking, and lid drumming.

Of the men I've known, you were the most steady,
reliable one near the window killing mosquitoes,
gathering cool water to press to my scalp. One-sided
heart I was then. Selfish one. I wanted everything.
Macaws flew past in quick flock, pushing outward
toward the earth's scattering filament and mystery.

*

I don't ask myself questions anymore
(*but it is not a question you ask yourself*),
rather the statement was born,
peeled like a film of dirt, (*rather...*
the words were meaning) wrapped inside
a scarf, stuffed into my carry bag, rather
that the camera caught all of it
(*the hunter and the kill*).

When danger itself was restless,
(*it had four legs and it ran with speed*
& vengeance) there was no purpose
(*though the past had nothing to do*
with the chase now). This beast stalking
(*pumped from its own engine of blood*),
centuries of evolution, first as a red-eyed
embryo, then reptile, then mammal, then
man, pure racing, push of muscle and tendon,
the tongue loose and dragging as the body
made its way forward. Each time more
powerful, a new version of waking until
the species grew great wings and lifted.

SO MUCH LIGHT WE COULD SEE TO THE OTHER SIDE

All fuel and fire, spine left like a bent arrow, dark matter,
the teeth as relic, all of our words bitter fruit. Who could
have believed we were made like this. The cosmonaut,

the soothsayer, and the blind archeologist knew merely
by feeling with the ends of their fingers which reached out
to nothing. We were a warring lot, hammered by days,

and greedy too. Our plates were dented with heavy spoons,
words spoken in secret in front of a fire, documents burned
before anything of substance was revealed. We made that fire,

fed the flames with newspapers, kings, martyrs, and love.
We were wanton, selfish, predisposed to constant dreaming.
We fed, fought and then fought some more until night arrived

with its hellish glow. All around us, mothers taught their children
words for the first time. They fashioned the universe into something
knowable, sayable. *Say this,* said the mother and the infant repeated

the words, clumsily, devoted. The child's devotion was the world
fabricating a truth. Repairs on the other side of the hemisphere.
The archeologist found our bones and said we were a strong

and healthy race, grew more ingenious than any generation before us,
before we fell away from wit, invention, our own empty embrace.
We ran to our end like leaping into a volcano. Unstoppable fury.

We should have disappeared entirely after the bomb, the floods,
our own desertion. Someone's mouth blows dust off the bones.
The soothsayer predicts that we will come back, the cosmonaut

is willing to bet when the world ended there were more
stars filling the sky than ever before. There once was shadow,
before a last light came, not to darken the plain but to define it.

POSSIBILITY

If you remember your place in this world
remember that you were restless meat,
that you were born four times: first as water,
then as a monk, then as an insect, then
a malleable distant star flicking *on, off, on*
in the child's insomniac eye.

When I was a girl, my mother's lover
bought me a small silver cross
in a bite-sized clear box and he took
me on his lap and I thought
he could be my lover too as I gestured
to kiss him on his lips.

I want what is beyond my reach,
blood red apple high in the trees,
where the sun threatens to harm it.
Late at night there are thorns in the bush.
I go unwarned as if I were predator,
threatening to take the world as my
own, to throw open its shutters.

The man sat still, letting the young girl
kiss him, then never came back.
This is how dark it can get, the heart says.
And the heart fasts for years until
it is lean. It shows its ribcage until
the soft apple falls into its dark patch.

STORY OF GIRLS

Years ago, my brothers took turns holding down a girl in a room.
They weren't doing anything to her but they were laughing and
sometimes it's the laughing that does enough. They held the girl down

for an hour and she was crying, her mouth stuffed with a small red cloth.
Their laughing matched her crying in the same pitch. That marriage
of sound was an error and the error kept repeating itself.

There were threats of putting her in the closet or in the basement
if she didn't quiet down. One cousin told them to stop but no one could
hear him above the high roar. After that the boy was silent, looking down

at his hands, gesturing toward the locked door. The mother was able
to push the door in and the boys were momentarily ashamed, remembering
for the first time that the girl was their younger sister. The mother ran

to the girl fearful that something had been damaged. Nothing was touched.
The brothers were merely dismissed as they jostled each other down
the long staircase. The girl sat up to breathe a little, then a little more.

Oftentimes it's the quiet cousin I think about.

FLESH ELEGY

Nude #1

The locusts are purring, zodiac turning
in the earth's celestial round as she took
her blouse to wrap around him, his boy's body
calmed past sleep, then zero. Boy's ear pressed
to his mother's chest, one missile, then two.
Once her bones detonated in a superior rush.
The glimmering was not false but a beckoning
not to be broken again, not to be a broken
lock, nor shattered dome, nor cracked cheekbone.
Then the smell of renovation, a staircase ascending,
the familiar ochre smell cindered up.

Nude #2

I was a prisoner locked into a mean definition
of myself, behind the tangle and shredded light.
I bent over the bucket, over switch and water,
electrified beyond myself, releasing over
the compound, shattering out. I think
now of the bleached owl I once saw flying very
low, inches from the dark ground, low enough
to bury itself before it rose lifting to the tallest
branch, execution and pinnacle.

Nude # 3

Standing on the idea's plateau, green, incessant.
Rising. Rebellion was set on earth. Hunger
utters: If you feed it once, it welcomes expectation.
If you feed it twice, it might love you. If you feed it
a third time, it will kill you for more. Reaching
the summit, she throws seed to the ground. The wild
descends to take from her hand: Vermin. Winter birds.
Torched field. We were welcomed into that face,
that fire, that dream whose simple life was foreign to us.

Nude #4

Insects mount the one bulb hanging
in an act of mating with lumen and burn.
She crawled all night. The mosquito
rearranges air with black buzz. It carries
an ancient life in its small carriage,
attaches itself to a distinct darkness.
Perhaps in another life it was mammoth,
conquering. When it pierces skin, bloodshed
in the name of the king, land overrun
by water, sound of oars moving back,
back, cradling time like a lover.

INTERPRETATION

I dream I am whipping a donkey
and I'm tired of whipping the donkey.
Its eyes yellowed and covered in a thin
film of mucous and it's not able
to take a step forward.

Love is breaking me. He comes
in the shape of a man blowing his nose
in the next room. Puddles of water
on the bathroom floor after he's showered,
and he's cold and I'm trying to feed
the both of us but I'm tired.

How many times can we fail before
we quit? I never quit. In my dream,
the donkey becomes a horse.
I ride the horse until the horse falls down,
then coax it with sweet talk and urging. I take
its mane and pull to make it run faster.

I've ridden the horse before this life;
it's charging through rivers, tearing
through desert, panting to arrive.
I've ridden the horse for so long
I have become the horse, the wind
heading up and out, breaking branches
with my night speed.

SOUND THAT IS A CAR SCREECHING,
A MICROPHONE TURNING ON

Your fingers were large around the pogo stick.
Fat child bouncing and bouncing along the sidewalk,
a great 1970s shadow stalking the streets. You wore
shorts too red, too short. You asked me three times
where my home was. I took a permanent picture of you.
I kicked the pogo stick to stop the action from running
its course. This is imagination running off the reel.
[Oh boy.] The pudgy fingers in the milk and in the batter.
The fudge on your face and Mother in an apron
loving with a blindness. Her red apron, your mouth
an alarm pulsing through the chocolate smear.
You were the last one I never wanted to love.
That push and pull, my skirt rising a little. [Oh.]
My temperature too. My shoes were red, the straps
a cocktail color too. Down the avenue, hula hoops
and double dutch swirling. I caught a shadow on
a barbed wire fence like a butterfly. It gasped
and gasped. I no longer remembered the minutes
before. My breathing slowed to tempo as its wings fell
a struggling flutter, then flat onto hot cement, a piece
of paper now sweating with the imprint of my lips.

HAUNTED

When ghosts walked in caverns overhead
no one believed me. Though there was a light
flashing all night. Though there was humming
in the woodwork. A man stood calling from inside
the well. I couldn't find him but I heard
his faint voice asking for me. From here,
I'm looking up into a very stark and real heaven
into a wide toothless mouth.

When the ghosts are ready, they shed their skin.
They take off their clear robes like falling water.
They examine my body X-rayed into a vision
from head to toe. The heart tunnels to its red core,
the parting of those curtains. The spine holds
me up like a ladder, my eyes two large rooms
preparing for greatness.

The ghosts are ready to step out on the brink
of my lips, onto the bright stage. They've always
been present, when I was afraid, when I did not
answer back. They spoke Latin, walked slowly
with baskets balanced on their heads. They sang.
I didn't hear for years, but now the house
is shifting from hip to hip.

My shoulders were tired but I walked further.
I made solemn vows that fell to the ground
like lost earrings. My lips were full with some
satisfaction about to spill through my teeth.
I had a handmade dress stitched with thread.
This may not sound special but it kept itself together.

I remember in my locked mouth an urge.
Ghosts through the doorway. Soul unraveling
at the seams but my hand expert, steady.
When I fashion the spirit, the lip goes here
and it's for telling, the eyes are hard black buttons,
the hand presses up to my century, cheek against
the glass pane during the first storm of my life,
my head lifting from the pillow, ghosts peering
through the keyhole, stalking my body, pushing
against my levity. But I am fixed to this earth,
a frozen salt flat, a hemisphere of crushed snow.

FORAGING AND DODGING

What does the stranger do but hold you
in this sleepless state, at the point
you were trying to leave your life?
What will happen once the storm
has come and gone, after paradise
is no longer paradise? Smell of him
like a broken bottle of wine.
We all want to be told something.
Me, I listen. A good woman can say
a lot. Signs along the way indicating
trouble: a bad temper, a horse shoe
print by the front door, seared
into the wood, a hidden pistol,
mace under a pillow. So much
to survive in this world. Your mother
is no longer alive and we can never
assume anything about anyone else's pain
though how do we live with
our knowledge? How the past
holds onto us with its short leash
and yelping.

We picked strawberries
by the highway and handed
them to each other, feeling
a weight. Toward the end
of her life, your mother
lived in a trailer by herself
just outside of town.

You might think that your life
is shatterproof, not prone
to breaking. Existence is a small
lit match hurled toward you.
You dodge it and smell smoke.
You dodge it and imagine
an alternate fate where fire
was at the very center.
You feel grateful, you breathe,
then walk away, whistling.

Some stories have a will
of their own. This one is not so happy.
Think of the horse shoe, the imprint
it made when thrown against
the door. Think of the woman
who dodges it and keeps loving
the man who threw it. Think of
her driving away in the night,
far from what she believes is devotion.
Her imagination was once in that house,
in the husband's weighted side
of the bed as he lay snoring.
Her imagination was the good food
she stirred on the stove, aroma
rising. This is called tension.
When you don't know what will
happen next, when the story
has a closed mouth, when it travels
forward or backward, when it
drives over a wooden bridge,

hearing the rush of the water
beneath, when it thrums to the thrum
of what is crashing inside,
it may sound like escape, it may
have blue blood, a beautiful
shut mouth, when it no longer
hides or lies to keep living,
when it misconstrues touch
for love, when it breathed
and found its rhythm, how
fruitful that day was, her body
shot through with light,
as she drove away, the bend
in the road coming into her
field of vision, as if life
loved her back, as if
she had a chance.

Neither evil nor kind, I walk the median.
Civilized, I talked to strangers, I looked
them straight in the eyes when I toasted
their future. I tried to teach invention
but it was difficult. I'm praising you
before the world turns on itself. Let
it be known that I betrayed myself
before I betrayed others, hid in the pews
so as not to be found. I had been wishing
for a better state of affairs, a way
of steadily climbing down the ladder.
My body looms, godly or ungodly.
I want to say something to your mouth,
filled with faith. The soul is dormant
in silence. The news is out, the space shuttle
hurtles toward earth. The findings
were not human but metal, surface.
With my machinery I worked on a vision
until it was blind, until I did not know
myself, until the shiver fell to splinters
and knew my name.

INFINITE AND PLAUSIBLE

It is the smallest idea born in the interior will,

that has no fury nor ignorance,

no intruder but stranger, no scaffold of a plea,

no mote of the hungry, no pitchfork of instinct,

no ladder of pity, no carriage of lust,

no wavering foot on concrete, no parish of bees,

no mountains of coal, no limestone and ash,

no lie poured down the stairs of a house among them,

and this is the will of maker and offspring,

no boot in the hallway indicating more exit

than arrival, more straying than strategy, no more struggle

than contained in my body now, as I wander the rooms,

tearing curtains apart from their windows

separating material from light.

LORD,

O beast, invisible flock,
leaves beneath the feet,
the flat crackling, bone,
hiss. The day was so fitful
it became a century. I took
down every last fence
with tools and all the lights
at the party.

There were three fires
in my lifetime and none
of them did any damage.
Each time, the pages turned,
singed with believing.
With that remorse,
I was free. I stood by
your faith, my father on
the other side, exchanging
one presence for the other,
speaking swiftly
to the legend of each.

And I came to know you,
understood the difficulty
in the backyard, learned
to feed myself as my own
guardian.

I am speaking into a bottle,
the sky at the end of it.
Since I was a child,

I valued beauty beyond
danger: prehistoric petals
pressed into the mouth
of a book, a doll with
a freshly painted face, a garden
out back buried in leaves.
I am speaking into the bottle,
meaning rising.

There's a strange light
coming over the mountain
but I'm not afraid anymore.
It is grey blue mottled
happiness that resembles
longing and I soak it up
with your bread.

III. Territory

TERRITORY

I do not hold myself responsible
to anything less than what I have done.

I have failed to tell you the truth.
These dark days a foreign number

placed on a boat set to sail. I promise
this is not my real face, but the one

I present to you in hiding, in a cell,
in a country beneath a wide, official

boot. Where does love exist
in this plain house shrouded in smoke?

Who lit the fire? What shelter
do I return to once the living is done?

A FULL LIFE

MODERN DAY ETHIOPIA, OGADEN DESERT

The devil takes stock of cans, food, rations
in the large factory. Takes out a roll of bandages
and a loaf of bread. If they ask for more, he orders
them to kneel, forces them to look at a wide expanse
of water or a table full of men eating, their tied women
on their laps. The devil is pulling a rope, feasting
on pork, wiping his face with the back of his face.

The rebels march 300 across
the crunchy earth. The entire village
lines up, one sunken cheekbone
to the next. Ethiopian soldiers
gang-raping women, burning down
huts and killing civilians at will.
It is the same military the American
government helps train and equip.

The devil likes to laugh and likes the women
to laugh too. *Laugh,* he says, when they are ordered
to shoot. *If you don't laugh, we'll shoot you too.* The devil
wears a mask with a hole for a mouth, painted cheeks
are shining silver dollars, eyebrows locked into their
official pallor. The mask is universal. The mask hangs
on the wall. When the devil sleeps, the mask still watches.

Lion. Radio. Fearless. Peacock.
Skimming water from the top
of a mud puddle, he pointed out
to the anthills, the coming storm clouds.
He said soldiers hanged his mother,
raped his sister, beat his father.

He'll turn to give a chance for escape but will club
the chest or feet. In the desert the women return
to their chores after the soldiers have left, arrange
their hair, and walk in circles looking for a body
of water, a surface in which to view themselves.

If I trust history, does my memory remain there?
What if the future fails me?

*

We have found it increasingly difficult to govern
our people. You, sitting with your toe touching water,
can you stir a whole continent by your jostling,
incessant questions: Is the pit of your stomach lifting
to your throat? Is the stomping more of a march
or a dance? What do you make of our new president?
Have you drunk our native wine? Aren't the women
of our country the most beautiful in the world?
Are you governed by saints or radicals? Should
I address you in the formal or the familiar?
When is curfew hour? When is the next plane
to New York? Do you carry bourbon or whiskey?

"A camel is delivering a baby today
and the milk of the camel is coming,"
goes one campfire song.
"Who is the owner of this land?"

*

The devil does not sit in a throne but in the brush
where he whispers to a soldier to take his share.
The soldier takes to dreaming and wishes
the terrain with its dominion of bird, beast,
women to be his. He dreams that he has 49
wives, the 50th will be his newborn daughter.

God set to fighting the devil with a sword.
In the year 2007, we can hear a clanging, not
in the heavens but in a backyard, not celestially,
but in the open mouth of a woman who watches
her daughter led into a room with soldiers.

The nation of Ethiopia is carrying me home.
I am carried home by this one long gospel
which seems to have no end, but I think
the final line may have something to do
with battling the one who made me.

IMAGINE, REFUGEE

Dream blood, dream red, dream.
The *r* and then the *ea* and the *m*.
Let the letters ride there, then subtract them.
The roof of a shelter, the grandeur
of smoke, a sun print on a rocket.

I have come to the border town.
Take away the *I* and place it in a shelter
dream, now fill it up with bullets, now
dream *bull*. Now take the *b* out of it
which is the engine that makes it go.

There's a baby in a basket.
There's a burning basket lullabye.
You know the words, mixed with soil
when the soil is lifted with a shovel.
Place the soil on top of the wooden boxes

whose bodies dream *ooh*'s and *aah*'s,
of fireworks branching out in the sky
on holiday, pots and pans clanging,
children playing at dawn, a dream
nailed down to a box.

SUBSTANTIAL

If I try to tell the truth, parachutes the size of fists
rain down in a territory in which they are not welcome.

If I live out my lies, I see a woman's sketched face
on the charcoal surface of a field where she

breaks apart on the pond's puzzle. I get on all fours,
low to the ground as if in an emergency.

I hide under desks, cover my ears, put on
a gas mask to look like a skeleton of an extinct insect.

Perhaps that was my ancestor's story and not mine
when the blast of sirens rang through the city. That sound

goes *left, left* along a heart-shifting latitude. Who is listening
if not me? All the words move individually orchestrating

a whole sound. It is as simple as a lone man wrapping
himself like a gift with a bomb at the center.

As simple as the next day when the streets are sanitized
and fruit again is being sold from baskets in the square.

Where are the people now? Why is the end so sharp when
I hold my hand in my hand? Maybe one day there will be a city

that crumbles from one great passion, and what will be left
is thieves, looters, thugs selling wares beneath my window.

All that will be left are blueprints of a once grand state,
a colossal loss standing like a ruined animal on one leg,

a face meant for breathing. Love is the mad pigeons,
ugly and ravenous, flying in blurred arcs over the city.

Land bleeding from a cut, tender face of the thick key
that opened the door to the inner song, color spreading

on the perfect wood floor creating the shape of danger,
its purpose to leave a mark, a stain.

PRAISE

for Haiti

All night long there was digging, and the bodies like accordions
bent into their own dying instruments, and even after this,

after the quake, there was, in news reports, still singing:
A woman's clapping was followed by another who shuffled

and dragged her own apparition through the ruined streets,
though each one knew the anthem the other was singing.

History taught them better. No one was coming.
The film crews had their sights on the large hotels,

the embassies. So they set to digging with their hands
and with the shoes of those who were no longer alive.

And with that, night fell and fell again
like an old black pot tumbling to the ground.

When a man dies, the first thing that goes is his breath,
and the last thing that goes is his memory.

I once saw this civilization passing through a great white door,
people weeping, then the weeping was followed by the sound

of tambourines rattling the air in a collision of ribbons
and bones, something that sounded like celebration

only livelier and more holy, voices rising, then a marching
into the dusty road of the next century. When shelter is gone,

find your solace on the ground. And when the ground is gone,
lift yourself and walk. And after all the great monuments

of your memory have collapsed, with the sky steady
above you, you shatter that too, with song.

IDENTITY

You, difficult engine.

    You, wide white plain

and north field.

You, bird of unknown origin

    your keen and quick flutter.

Lightning penetrates the ocean,

split and gutted, solarized,

    shining for seconds.

The sound knows its matching sound

and shuts itself in noiselessly.

    Profile of you in black and white,

before catastrophe and after bliss.

The shutter and the opening,

    I know you.

The backlight as you rise

this morning shades the ether.

    You, a stunning blur.

You, mortal without a face.

MORTAL TETHER

It was slavery. Going backward in time,
the order to build a large fire by rubbing
my hands together without end. I'm fighting
them off with billy clubs. The heart's heavy
shift makes a screech when it turns
from the past. What is that essential blackness,
cables holding me up over this air and history?
During escape, were we brave enough to climb
that steep hill, when our faces were painted
for camouflage, running away from firestorm,
from gunshot and dog? Each time I looked
at the eclipse, it had a difficult face. I fastened
myself to you in colorized film, your mouth
tied to my shoulder, biting into areas
meant for harnessing because sometimes
I climbed too high and I didn't want
to come back. But you steadied me with
your grasp and mortal tether. A power switch,
blinking bulbs, the awakening. Years ago
we would have been whipped in separate
chambers, your teeth digging into my skin
that grew out of a girl's body ages ago.

LABOR

My handwriting is rough, a prisoner's scripted
letter, the cropped fields and your winter palms
folding into my pockets for lack of gloves.

I could go in any direction in this field of nocturne.
They place fistfuls of pebbles in my shoes.
A message stuck in someone's mouth.

I wander after ancestry, in long brocade,
in tattered coat. Does the voice call
from shrapnel and dung, wood and smoke?

Do I begin in this past, the famine field?
My mother once knew nothing but snow
but knew it was made from cold,

and its opposite: ash, splinter, ruin.
From that fire, came a long winter.
I am guided now by a river

but I cannot return to that state of water.
It is a tale. That love might save.
They took away another prisoner yesterday.

I hear a wrestling, a drag from that deep,
a face rippling in the undercurrent.
I don't remember the struggle.

I am landlocked, no more responsible
for my own body. I am summoned
into the new year by firecrackers,

a detonation, a good luck orange bursting
from its hot center. I wonder
how I've come to surrender, settle

into the blind familiar. It is not a revolution,
when I get to admit my mistakes,
when I wear my wrongs like a shining badge,

where my confessions lead me
to a final world. In the morning,
my soaked bread a slumped body.

WHEN THE WAR WAS IMAGINARY

I did not have a gun and did not want to use it.
Not once for intruders. Not once near the border.
I am a soldier, shouldering rain.
I am a soldier in the sun, wearing a hard hat.
When my mouth opens, I wag my tongue.
I have a gun and it talks with a low voice.

I love you. We drowned in water, I let the dam go
and I shot the gun, bullets swimming toward you,
your mouth open to kiss me. It was gorgeous.
That moment we met, we imagined
there was peace. When the shots hovered
in the water, bright bullets tangled in your hair.

A FULL LIFE

MODERN DAY SRI LANKA, JAFFNA

The nights are broken by artillery fire across
the black lagoon: Fever in the white stone garden:
By 7 p.m., stray dogs have the run of Jaffna's streets:
An animal in the outer quarters grinds the minutes
with hind teeth: *The city's people are indoors before*
8 o'clock curfew: Time in a bowl, lapped up.

Soldiers linger at the edges of the valley:
A man is called a scavenger in 40 languages:
At least 15,000 are waiting to get on government ships:
A sure existence of heaven or hell but not both:
to the relative safety of Colombo, the capital:
This is Jaffna, the picturesque prize of Sri Lanka's

ethnic civil war, girding for a new storm: You can't
have the angel's wing and the demon talon too:
No other place in Sri Lanka is so scarred because
no other place carries Jaffna's special curse:
There is a line that begins in the first minute
of the world: *a homeland that the Tamil Tigers*

have fought to carve out: and ends with my present
desire: *the trophy the soldiers and rebels*
have fought over for nearly 25 years. The nameless
bird from nowhere calls: *It is no stranger to war:*
Its temples and churches bear the pockmarks
of battles past: All night it charges through

a world: *A new fear stalks Jaffna, more ominous*
than any its people recall from the past: its body
disappearing but only its stirring remains: *mysterious*
abductions usually carried out during curfew hour:
All night it scatters the earth with seed, water gurgling
a manifesto, a haunting army of goodbyes:

No one is quite sure who is being taken:
long sleeves caught in the lower branches:
for what reason, by whom: No more a kind
of grieving than happiness is: *Sometimes, bodies*
turn up on the street: Listen to that inhuman moan:
More often, they do not turn up at all:

It speaks in a language you consider foreign,
primitive: *In January, a university student was plucked*
from his village, taken to what he later identified
as a series of military camps: Your refusal to come outside
hurts it: *He said his captors hung him upside down*
from the ceiling and beat his feet: You're rummaging

for lock and key, searching for small tools
to fend off disaster: *They covered his head with*
a plastic bag soaked in gasoline: Human, let
the ghost split, let it jangle the leaves
like jewelry in their green: *They rammed*
a stick into his anus: Heart wailing to the bone:

After seven days, they left him on the side of a railway track:
Let the world fly, estranged tongue, common language:
He maintains that he has no links to the rebels: Love is a lie.
I should have told you that in the beginning: *Not far
from the general's office, 300,000 people who have been misplaced
by the conflict:* Love spins inward into a helix at the beginning

of time: *Food aid has not come for weeks. Women have sold
their gold bangles for rice:* You can never fix this history.

THE EMPRESS DOWAGER CONTEMPLATES HER LINEAGE

I feel drowned in abundance, my wild boys
in the fountain, my food, and every last dog
in the pack. Look at my face, loveless horses

near the pond, a shipwreck of bone.
And what is beauty now but a sterile stitch
in my pose. It was vicious rising.

This is my confession: My murdering bunch
was in the commons. I cover this secret
with a sweep of rouge. Yesterday, my portrait

was taken as I looked to the west. I hitched myself
to a higher star. When my eyes were blinking
toward industry, I thought of the daughter

I will not have. I believe she would have been
a weak songstress. I would have crushed her
like a pill. Listen to rain fall in every territory.

My story is not my own, but history's.
When I'm restless, I think of the bucket
with the shallow water, where I drowned her,

twisted her into a knotted tree that grew
in the netherworld. She would have been
a meek girl. One with bones I could eat.

TO EMPRESS: BY DAY

Soldier:

It's the hand died fabric that slides dazzling
green as if you were born into the world
in cool calm, in a whirl of being more than a peasant's
daughter. In another time, you would have been worth
nothing, not even hired to sheer my whiskers
or tie my boot strings. But no matter what era,
you close in on a man with a razor, with a willingness
to cut what stands in your way. Woman, you tell me
each secret by whispering behind your open hand,
following it with a laugh as if it made it less significant,
more a passing remark than the fall of the chopping knife.

I have seen you in nightmares, with men on leashes.
Each time I asked you to get on your knees
you wore a half smile punching a lipstick mark
on my collar. Today I conquered a nation for you,
crumbled cities only to reach you here. Guilt
never touched your lips, your hands never dirtied,
washed with rainwater, food tasted for you,
a final gesture hidden in your robe,
poison in a wine chalice fashioned for an extinct king.

Empress:

I was just a peasant standing with a skirt full of starfruit,
my baby crying in the makeshift cradle, hidden
in straw. I was a mother once and then I wasn't.
I had whole pieces of food in my hand,
so fresh, they burned me. When the smoke rose,
the volcano threatened to erupt. When the plates
shifted below me, I thought the world's green was gone.

In celebration ribbons fly, grazing ground, carried
by wind. You, on other side of those gates.
It must have been the company, halls full of people
crowding. The strange clinking of glasses was a screech,
sign of joy. The food was perfect, salty enough to sting.
In the center of my lips, you, dark to taint me.

REIGN

The empress dowager was fourth in line,
peeled from her clothing, placed
at the foot of the emperor's bed.

Should she have a weapon, she would have
no clothes to conceal it, her long fingernails
as sex toy or talon.

Bearing a son, she was promoted.
The eunuchs conspired with her.
She ruled the country and didn't want

anything back but jewels cutting into
everything. When the emperor died, her son
was next in line; he sought whores, opium

until he died too. She was left in power
with her vaults of gems gleaming.
She loved the poached eggs in the golden bowl,

the hundred dishes on lacquer plates.
She was beautiful once
and beauty made her master.

Dot of lipstick on her mouth, bitten red,
the walk through the walled city, the willful
assassination of love, the famine

which fed her, made her want nothing more
from her own kind. She looked at the mirror,
a hollowed face watching the monsoons

sweep away the houses in the heat.
The weeds rose up through her body,
breaking her, tearing through.

She loved once, a theater of fantastic concerns.
The sky was a careful picture
and she paid one hundred artists to get it right.

Locked in a windowless room, they imagined clouds
searing through solid mountain. She had all killed
but one. She paid the best architect in the country

to make her room something from a page in heaven
so that when she opened her door, she could swear
she was dying in riches dripping from her living hand.

A century later when they dynamited her grave,
her teeth were still intact, her expression pure,
paramount, nostrils and mouth stuffed with diamonds.

LOVE, OVER

I say it is brown.
The color of soil,
the color of an iris,
the color of your hair
as I combed through it.

I arrived on the other side,
sweat still on my body.
My body is a language
I'll sing to you
sometimes off key,
pure violation,
pure penance,
pinnacle, accident.

In Manila, 32 hours
after I departed
New York, you hold
a sign with my name
waiting for me quietly
in the heat.

We meet the vice mayor
who holds a bottle of beer
behind his back. Your cousin
shows me a gun and a stack
of Rolex watches splayed
on the card table.
His daughter cries
on the linoleum floor,
spinning herself in circles.

At the market, mackerel
in a blue plastic basin,
swimming and flopping
onto the hot ground.
What was to save
after this particular fate?

When they split the goat
open, the animal
is not red inside
but brown, cushioned
by a little noise,
then noiseless.

SUCCESSION

I am channeling a beginning but something has to end first.
Was there wind beyond? What floated on that current?

There's a cave inside me. An entry with a clear opening
but no hinges. You must walk into it without fear of losing.

The bats hang in their winged houses, icicles in their clear shapes
dripping downward. If you go inside it requires patience

and compassion to get there and a belief that you will not
be lost. I apologized as I entered. I sat among the rocks

and limestone when I made it through the labyrinth,
when the universe outside settled into a low murmur.

It took discipline not to move from my place, my home
under the gypsum and fracture. But fortune had its uniform.

It was looking for me with torch light and cool calling.
I pretended not to hear, though I recognized its need

to find me there, my teeth glowing from my coal face,
a future shining from the void.

BRIGHT ORDER

When you died, you were shot in both eyes,
a vision of blindfolded saint, and even then
we couldn't agree on which one. A simple burial:
your belongings placed into the pit of earth,
burning the surface in a circle of fire.

Wandering a labyrinth in the netherworld,
you asked for money to make it to the next
invisible city. When your mother kissed you,
you surrendered to an immaculate moment
that even god had not anticipated. That memory
grew and you thought of her as they roped you
upside down, your body swinging like a bell.

THE DOWAGER MEETS ME IN THE PRESENT

(BROOKLYN, 2010)

Dowager:

Toward my death all my men, steely and silent,
lined up before me with their complicated faces.
Each with a gift: a hairpin, a beehive of golden leaves
but one I remember most, swell of fabric from
an orphan's dress. This a peasant offered
and I didn't know why he wept for me, I who
gave him nothing. A swirl of light stormed
in my chest and gathered like a plea.

I:

I never cared for history with its mistakes, its blurbs,
its great attempts at summary, its masters and migrants
and figurines stacked in witness though here you are,
studded, stubborn, magnificent on a bridge between
boroughs. You are a marionette with a dialect
of persuasion. One day I took my last drink and the fog
cleared. I saw in the mirror a blue heron breaking
the dome sky before it plummeted head first into
the lake of me. What rose was something like you:
Mostly magic, mostly majestic with an intuition
to possess. I rounded the corner burning, to arrive
at my life where I leaned between traffic light
and avenue, between gate and shelter.

Dowager:

Once there were many gods in a very small town.
All male. None of them brave. From each continent
they courted and asked that I offer my East
as dowry. I thought of grain, gold, spice. I pondered
oxen, tea, onyx and gave none. I laughed
as a fitful cat, pushed them a thimbleful of drink.
I slept with a different god each night. I performed
backflips, ordered shadows to kneel against the wall,
miniature people shaking and shuddering.
Even my feet were precious, toes adorned with sugar
and diamond dust. I let them crawl bellies dragging
ground while I hovered behind a screen, fastening
an earring, brushing the length of my hair, follicles
falling like spent bodies in heaps around me.

I:

I'm not sure if I can invoke it: Laughter
on the porch steps. A bombing. A beginning.
Which beginning is not Myth? Not Bible?
Not Koran? It is 4:00 a.m. on an empty street.
The sanitation trucks drone an alternate
American song, one-sided conversation
of discard, holy dog fuel, incessant trash.
Chiseled stone, a message wedged at the back
of my throat, revelers dance in the courtyard
vowels break open from their sacred cartridges.

Dowager:

How many times did I weary in my private room
as someone nursed my lone son. Future god rising
like a bald moon beneath a breast. How man times
did he bellow beneath my train of fabric, hide
behind those sheer curtains. He was ailing all the time.
I wore him like a brooch. He spoke when I asked,
sparkled when he opened his mouth to eat
from me, cry like a steel trap.

I:

I was dismantled as though through the jaws
of a great modern machine, industry moving a woman
through its wheels with spark and sputter as I
obliged, cursed back. My resistant mouth opened
for a fuse to be lit but it was not the suspected voices
of angels, creamy arms rising up. It was a parade
where girls poured from their own hips, bell, drum
and wine. Here, every siren is parked under a tree,
every siren a mess of blood on sidewalks, cars rally
the revelers. There are guns in the present,
in these blue pockets. But by morning the ruptures
are healed, heavens heaving.

Dowager:

Unleashing myself I become a legion of panther
scattering after buffalo, rampaging after coyote,
all of me biting into an interior spirit, the mirror
image of teeth. I love nothing but the devouring,
the young ones running.

Come to me in this made bed. This space between us
only instinct, craving. Here, nothing marks time
but time. I am that undercurrent sensation,
that discomfort from century to century that keeps you
questioning, keeps you both fixed and fidgeting.
If you summon a belief it becomes truth. All the gods
are an utterance, an Amen in any language. I name you
Daughter. My only one. There are no gods. There are
many gods. Which face is lying and is half of it yours?

THE IDEA OF REVELATION

It wasn't holy so let us not praise gods.
Let us not look to them for bread,
nor the cup that changed water to wine.

Let us look to the bend of the road
that reaches. A silver blur across
the skyline, woman standing on the farm.

In her grasp, the shine that is seed,
that is beginning. She will work
the earth, bounty in the vault

of cosmos above her, heat
lightning that lassoes in its manic
current. Man never existed

but to invite danger. Loveless one.
There was once an army of men,
saluting from bayonet to bomb.

They were expert at sabotage, hand combat.
You stop the clock in your paltry chest.
The one that says *choose, choose.*

Wind that desired backward. Ring
the alarm. When you wake, no more
pain. A mirror like a window looking out.

What can your past now say to you
that has never been said before? What
of that clock that forbade you to move

forward. What of the clock that asked
for nothing but passage, the minutes
careening into you like a fitful arrow.

What of the clock that summoned nothing,
not even mercy. Once you tired of wanting,
a face to break, you started the clock again.

CELESTIAL

When everything was accounted for
you rummaged through my bag to find
something offensive: a revolver,
a notebook of misinterpreted text.

I'm God's professor.
His eyes two open ovens.
He has a physical body
and it hiccups and blesses.

Tell me a story before the mudslide,
tell it fast before the house falls,
before it withers in the frost, before
it dozes off next to the television.

I couldn't tell if it was that screen
or the sky spitting dust and light.

STRANGE GOD,

Where was that stairwell that led up?   Where was

                that furnace that burned the face of a picture

of a father + a daughter in the snow?   The frost melted

                  inches from me. The mouths shone
through the silver.

I can feel your hand moving darkly

        then brightly over the plain.   Twitching.

Darkness falls down

deep into the well where I take my clean water.

                  The shelter was wood.

It was high-beamed + hiding me. It was dripping,

           canopied.

Strange God, I understand the human void. Because there is an avalanche

        hesitating
           before the crush. Because

this car drives away from land. The mirror, a view of the road, leading away.

I turned to the furnace whose opening   looked to me

                    + I returned its stare

which spoke loss, spoke departure then arrival.

The crow flying over the green lawn is not an omen

                    but a force of opposites,

                                        my longing moves

                    along in degrees.

                    Back in the city

when you touched me, water fell out of a faucet   + filled

          a glass that balanced under the opening.

Father + Strange God, over the rooftop the cardinals are dressed in fog.

The birds have been rummaging in my breastbone

          hard at work, searching for meat.

God + Father, my friend brought a meal,

          a chicken cooked + steaming to a woman who had nothing.

The woman took the chicken

    + cracked the chest in half with her broad hands

without effort, just need.

EPILOGUE

In civilizations past, I would have been worshipped,
not as a queen but as the soul's accident.
The archeologists brushed the bones of dust
and worm, and placed their magnifying glasses
to the specimen, eyes as large as planets
as they examined me, a small crack in a vessel.
They whispered among themselves before they lifted
the remains, placed them by a small fire hoping
the remnants would catch the light. Perhaps it is
prophecy or history's faulty memory. They caught
my brittle life, my tribe of people vanishing.

NOTES

The Empress Dowager who was also known as *Tzu Hsi, Cixi,* and the *Empress Dowager of the West* was the last empress of China, and ruled from 1861 until her death in 1908. Though some facts have been attained from Sterling Seagrave's *Dragon Lady* and other historical sources, it must be noted that many details in the poems are acts of invention in order to create a mythological life of the Empress.

"Unfinished Book of Mortals" is after the poem "Unfinished Book of Kings" by W. S. Merwin.

"Charlatan, Self-Styled" is borrowed from one of Sterling Seagrave's subtitles.

"Flesh Elegy" is after the poem "The Glass Essay" by Anne Carson.

"A Full Life: Modern Day Ethiopia, Ogaden Desert": Italicized portions are from "Searing Reports Back a Rising U.S. Worry" by Jeffrey Gettleman, *The New York Times*, June 18, 2007.

"A Full Life, Modern Day Sri Lanka, Jaffna": Italicized portions are from "Sri Lanka's Scars Trace Lines of War Without End" by Somini Sengupta, *The New York Times*, June 15, 2007.

"Infinite and Plausible" is after the poem "Necessary and Impossible" by Henri Cole.

1. In a dream city constructed from paper, flames were lit. My God, I am the Japanese beetle green and shining in front of the dark door. World, I grieve into your small, disinterested ear. I am quivering inside a thousand rooms of one cell, where I hover and freeze, black as a speck descending the far, blank page.

2. My love feeds me green mangoes to remind me of Baguio. He unwraps tamarind candy and places it on my tongue. He forgives me all the times I've lost my temper, spilled liquor, dented doorways. He laces my delicate shoes up my legs, kisses me on the knees. Down the road, it's raining. Water through the tall trees. School children walk in rows, holding palm leaves over their heads. I'm like my own history before me: I ruin. My heart's soggy existence. I want to name everything in this world. Even objects that have gone extinct. I name all the birds so I can call them one by one. Red is the color of blood, paper money, and luck. When the ghost money burns smoke rises to meet me, like his phantom shape, identical to the love I heave on my back.

3. In a Chinese picture book, the cartoon girl is feeding a deer and the deer wanders away and she hurts herself. The Chinese character for moon hangs with one hook drawn above her and the strokes of the word fall down in sheets. Fury is what she's after. The heap on the ground she walks toward is the brush stroke of the moon, swollen like a body and she brushes earth and the sound of the river away from her ear. I've known love, angry river rushing past. Afterward, there are bright lists of things in my hands: a rock, diamond, a shining document. I know that girl and I know the last of her story. How she grew up and unlaced herself from her corset. Found the deer and knelt down beside it. Opened the animal when no one was looking.

4. She had no use for God. What, then, was the use of praying? This god bled so easily, pity dripped to the floor. Music drifted from the church radio. Weeks later he played that same music for her in his room while her stockings dried on his bedpost, his windowsill.

5. This poem began centuries ago. This poem will soon find its end. Those sounds late at night could have been ghosts or my old soul calling me back, passed through the walls and landing before me. The buildings ahead of me have toppled and the kettle on the stove whistles, waits for a presence to silence it.

6. If this is my last letter, perhaps it is not important to write it beautifully, but strangely. To catch the ear off guard, to hook you by the sweater, an arm, a mouth. I send it to you, without stamp, without envelope or paper. I place my faith in it, alphabet unwritten, tattered correspondence of wind. Some people were faithless, as they built a bridge with string, with wood. I had my love run toward you in rivulets of water. I faced south and forgot my fury. The words write themselves, the pen dips in ink at night. I am civilization. I am loneliness. Beyond boundary, rebel country, past the plain destined for battle, littered with refugees. Love, I think I see you in the dark's dark with your whole hooves pounding. When you come to me, you do so after years of travel, and arrive at the other end of my hand, untethered, your shining body, feral, a wild belief returning to me.

ACKNOWLEDGMENTS

Sincere thanks to the editors of these publications in which the following poems or earlier versions appeared:

Academy of American Poets (www.poets.org), *Barrow Street, drunkenboat, Gathering of the Tribes, Guernica: A Journal of Art and Politics, Lumina, McSweeney's, The New York Times, Ploughshares, PEN World Voices.*

"Celestial" appeared in Poem-A-Day, www.poemflow.com/768, iPhone app for the Academy of American Poets.

"Praise," appeared in *The Brooklyn Paper* and on www.brooklyn-usa.org, the website of the Brooklyn Borough President.

"The Empress Dowager Dreams After a Poisoned Meal" appeared in *A Face to Meet the Faces: An Anthology of Contemporary Persona Poetry*, edited by Stacey Lynn Brown and Oliver de la Paz.

Gratitude to the Blue Mountain Center, The Constance Saltonstall Foundation, the Djerassi Artist's Residency, the Virginia Center for the Creative Arts, as well as Lara Held and Justin Key for the gift of time, nourishment, and shelter in the wild. The Academy of American Poets, The Asian American Writers' Workshop, Cave Canem, the Poetry Society of America, Poets House for community and collaboration. To Mark Doty for his luminous spirit and support from the beginning. Peter Covino, Eric Gamalinda, Timothy Liu, Tracy K. Smith for their close and sensitive reading of these poems. To the borough of Brooklyn who accepted me and nurtured me and great thanks to Marty Markowitz and his wonderful staff for having faith in me as their next laureate. Ongoing thanks to Martha Rhodes, Ryan Murphy, Sally Ball and the Four Way staff for believing in my work and ushering this book to completion. The New York Foundation for the Arts provided funding crucial for sustenance during the writing process. For love and guidance my friends: Amy, Jennifer, Judy, Lara, Nathalie, Ravi, Robin. Deep thanks to my family for their continued belief and support. Special gratitude to Claude De Castro whose magic and gifts prompted me to write many of these poems. To Juliette and Roman who taught me that inspiration and bliss are within my reach.

ABOUT THE AUTHOR

Tina Chang was raised in New York City and is currently Brooklyn Poet Laureate. She is the author of *Half-Lit Houses* (Four Way Books, 2004) and co-editor of the anthology *Language for a New Century: Contemporary Poetry from the Middle East, Asia, and Beyond* (W.W. Norton, 2008). Her poems have been published in *American Poet*, *McSweeney's*, *Ploughshares*, and *The New York Times*, among others. She has received awards from the Academy of American Poets, the Barbara Deming Memorial Fund, the Ludwig Vogelstein Foundation, the New York Foundation for the Arts, Poets & Writers, and the Van Lier Foundation among others. She teaches poetry at Sarah Lawrence College and is an international faculty member in the MFA Creative Writing Program at the City University of Hong Kong, the first low-residency MFA program to be established in Asia.

WITHDRAWN
No longer the property of the
Boston Public Library.
Sale of this material benefits the Library